MODERN CLASSIC SONATAS

BOOK 2

Dr. Anis I. Milad

authorHOUSE®

AuthorHouse™
1663 Liberty Drive
Bloomington, IN 47403
www.authorhouse.com
Phone: 1 (800) 839-8640

*"This book "Modern Classic Sonatas - Book 2" includes sonatas which were composed by Dr.
Anis I. Milad. Dr. Milad expressed his emotion and was able to complete each sonata in three parts
"exposition, development, and recapitulation" and in a variety of Key Signature. These sonatas
are also published in YouTube. Producing books to include this form of music is a door for the new
generations to follow and improve the classic music. This book is also produced to get the attention of
the conductors and the musicians around the world to our world in the United States of America"*

Published by AuthorHouse 07/11/2019

ISBN: 978-1-7283-1889-9 (sc)
ISBN: 978-1-7283-1890-5 (e)

Contents

Sonata No 11, Op 62 - The Uncertainty of the Finish Line

Dr. Anis I. Milad

Sonata No 11, Op 62 - The Uncertainty of the Finish Line

Sonata No 11, Op 62 - The Uncertainty of the Finish Line

Sonata No 12, Op 64 - The Waltz of Poverty

Dr. Anis I. Milad

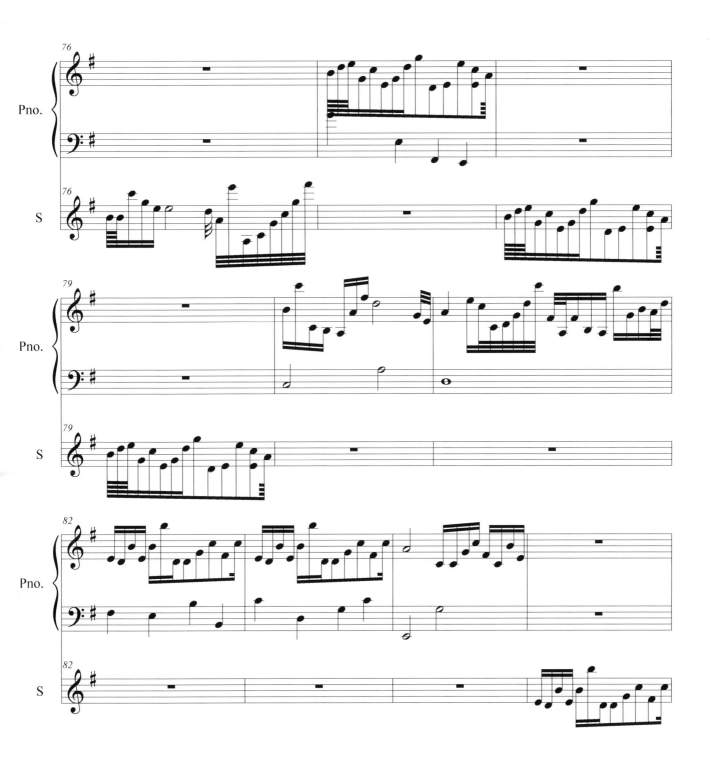

Sonata No 12, Op 64 - The Waltz of Poverty

44

Sonata No 12, Op 64 - The Waltz of Poverty

Sonata No 12, Op 64 - The Waltz of Poverty

Sonata No 12, Op 64 - The Waltz of Poverty

Sonata No 12, Op 64 - The Waltz of Poverty

Sonata No 12, Op 64 - The Waltz of Poverty

Sonata No 12, Op 64 - The Waltz of Poverty

Sonata No 12, Op 64 - The Waltz of Poverty

Sonata No 12, Op 64 - The Waltz of Poverty

Sonata No 12, Op 64 - The Waltz of Poverty

70

Score

Sonata No 13, Op 65 - The Other Religion Discriminate Not

Dr. Anis I. Milad

Sonata No 13, Op 65 - The Other Religion Discriminate Not

Sonata No 13, Op 65 - The Other Religion Discriminate Not

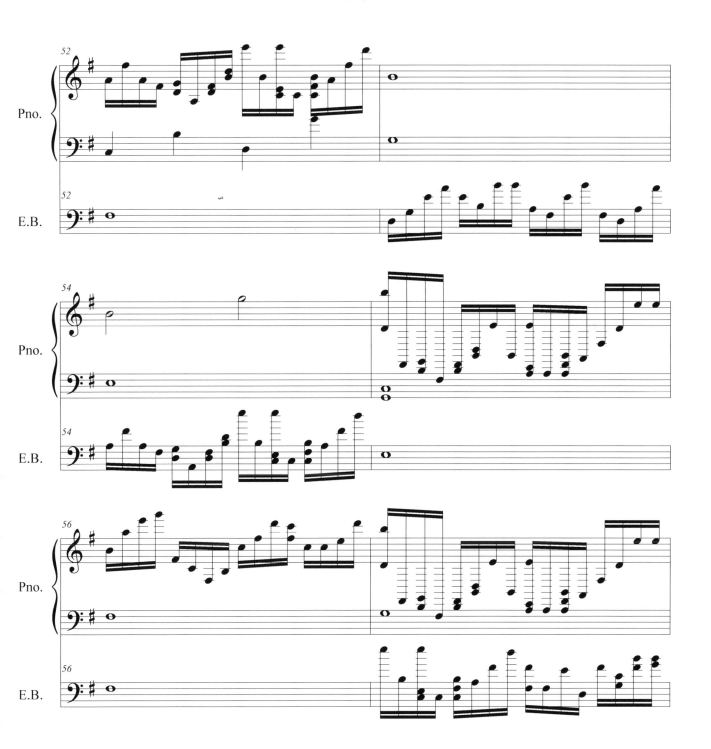

Sonata No 13, Op 65 - The Other Religion Discriminate Not

Sonata No 13, Op 65 - The Other Religion Discriminate Not

104

Sonata No 14, Op 68 - My God, My God, Why Not?

Dr. Anis I. Milad

Sonata No 14, Op 68 - My God, My God, Why Not?

Sonata No 14, Op 68 - My God, My God, Why Not?

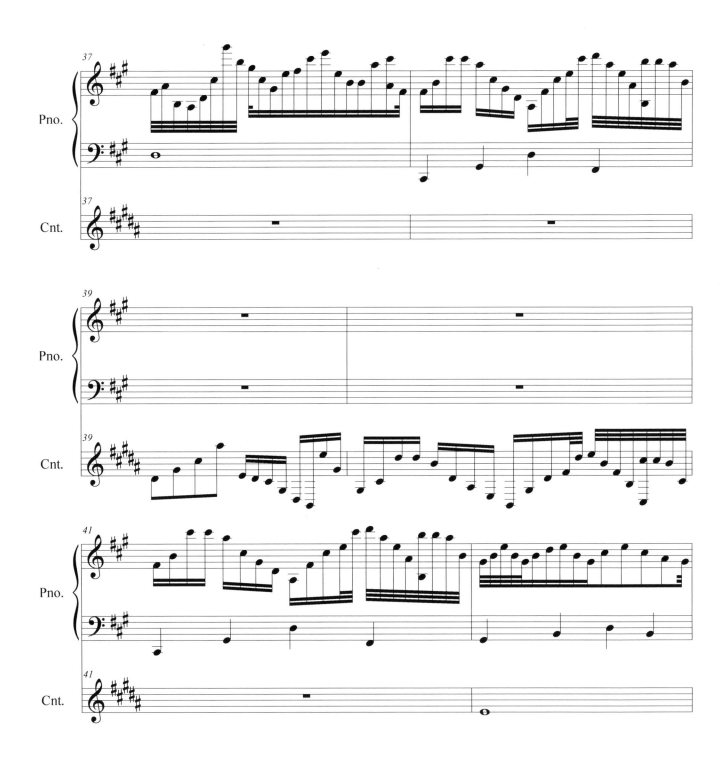

Sonata No 14, Op 68 - My God, My God, Why Not?

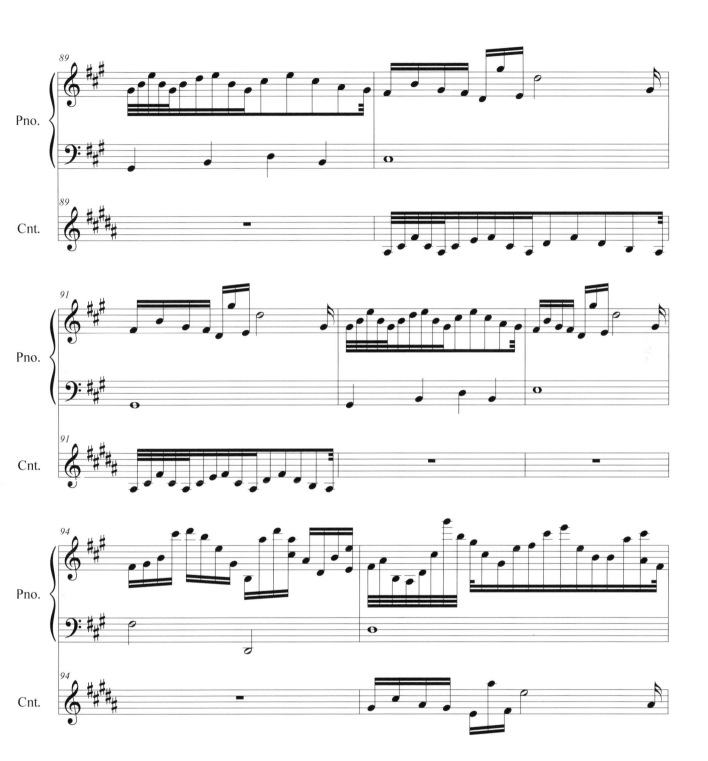

Sonata No 14, Op 68 - My God, My God, Why Not?

Sonata No 14, Op 68 - My God, My God, Why Not?

Sonata No 14, Op 68 - My God, My God, Why Not?

126

Sonata No 14, Op 68 - My God, My God, Why Not?

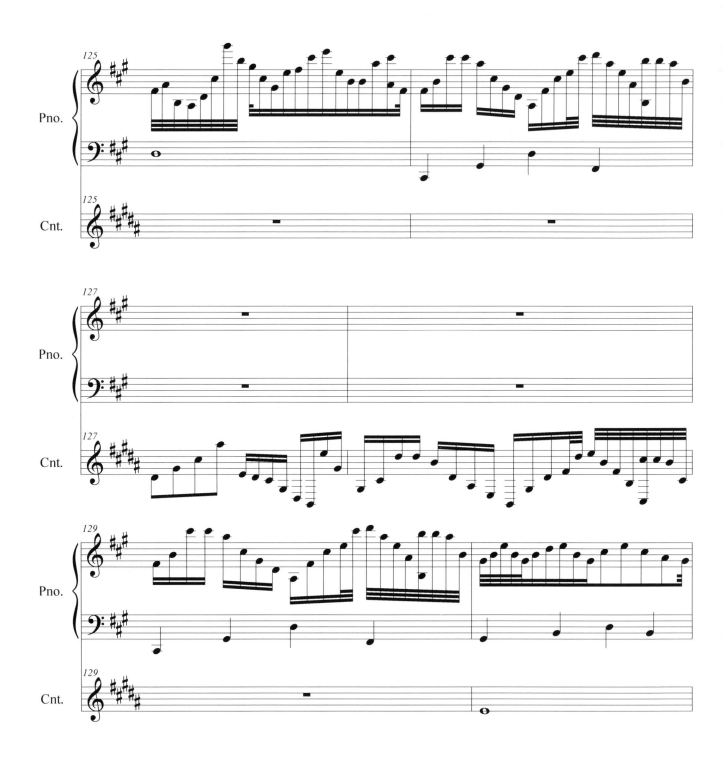

Sonata No 14, Op 68 - My God, My God, Why Not?

Sonata No 14, Op 68 - My God, My God, Why Not?

130

Sonata No 14, Op 68 - My God, My God, Why Not?

Sonata No 14, Op 68 - My God, My God, Why Not?

Sonata No 14, Op 68 - My God, My God, Why Not?

135

Sonata No 14, Op 68 - My God, My God, Why Not?

Sonata No 14, Op 68 - My God, My God, Why Not?

138

Sonata No 14, Op 68 - My God, My God, Why Not?

Sonata No 14, Op 68 - My God, My God, Why Not?

Sonata No 14, Op 68 - My God, My God, Why Not?

Sonata No 14, Op 68 - My God, My God, Why Not?

Sonata No 14, Op 68 - My God, My God, Why Not?

146

Sonata No 14, Op 68 - My God, My God, Why Not?

150

Sonata No 14, Op 68 - My God, My God, Why Not?

Sonata No 14, Op 68 - My God, My God, Why Not?

Sonata No 14, Op 68 - My God, My God, Why Not?

Sonata No 14, Op 68 - My God, My God, Why Not?

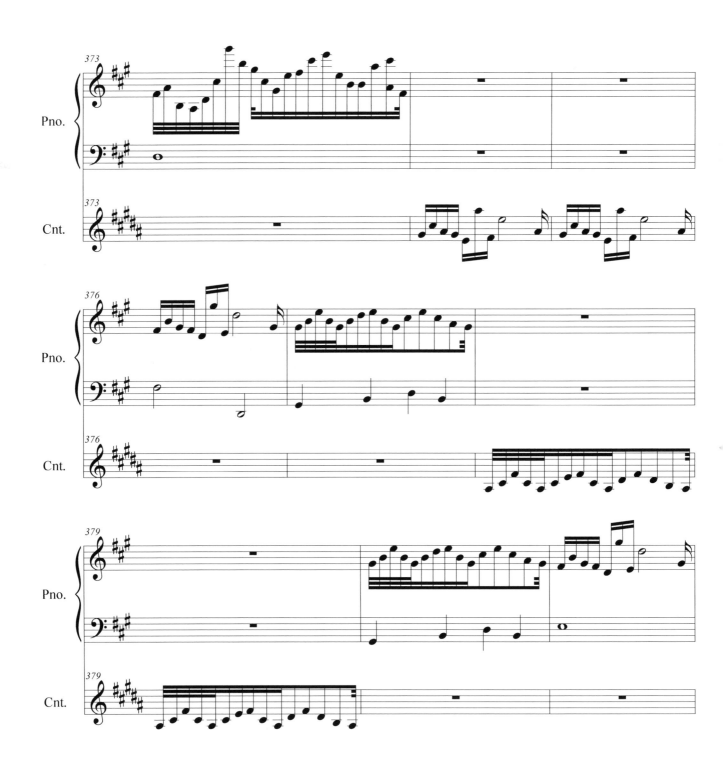

Sonata No 14, Op 68 - My God, My God, Why Not?

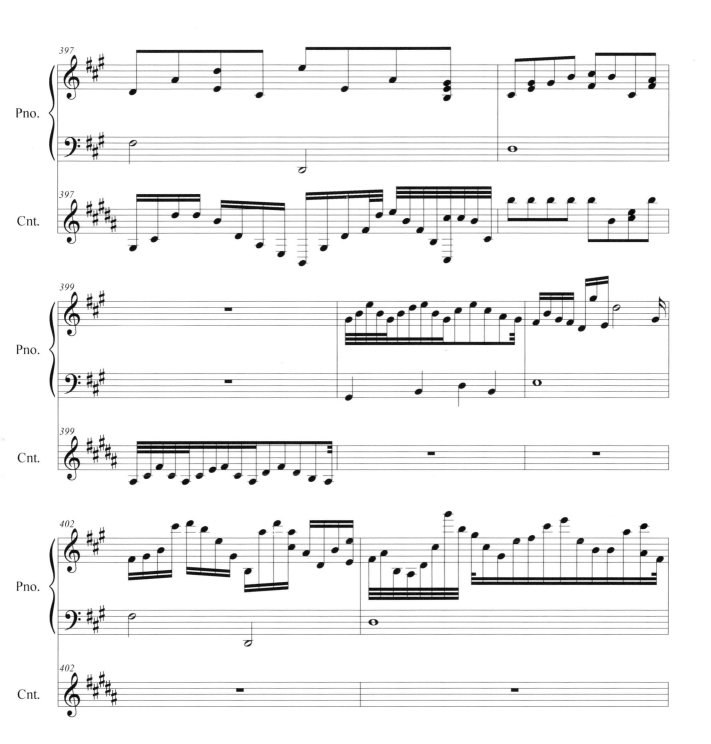

159

Sonata No 14, Op 68 - My God, My God, Why Not?

162

Sonata No 14, Op 68 - My God, My God, Why Not?

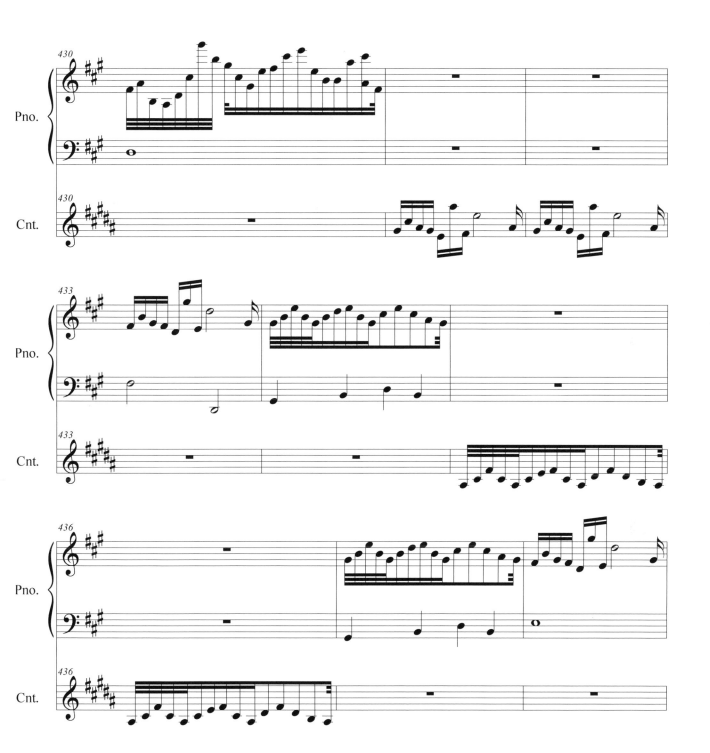

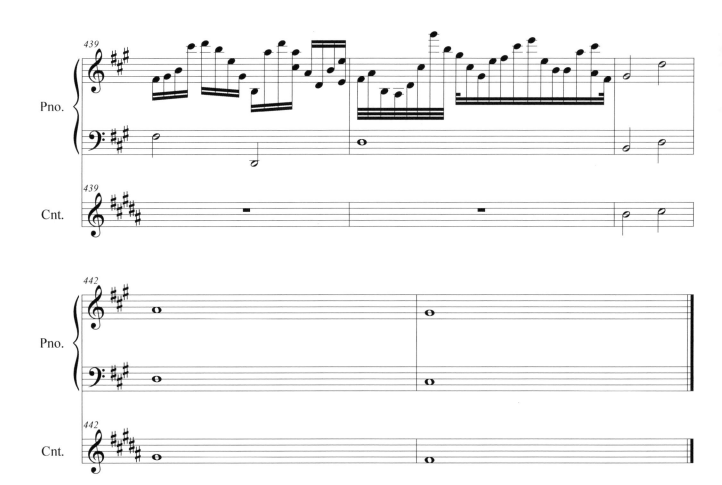

Sonata No 15, Op 70 - Broken Heart

Dr. Anis I. milad

Sonata No 15, Op 70 - Broken Heart

Sonata No 15, Op 70 - Broken Heart

172

Sonata No 15, Op 70 - Broken Heart

173

Sonata No 15, Op 70 - Broken Heart

Sonata No 15, Op 70 - Broken Heart

176

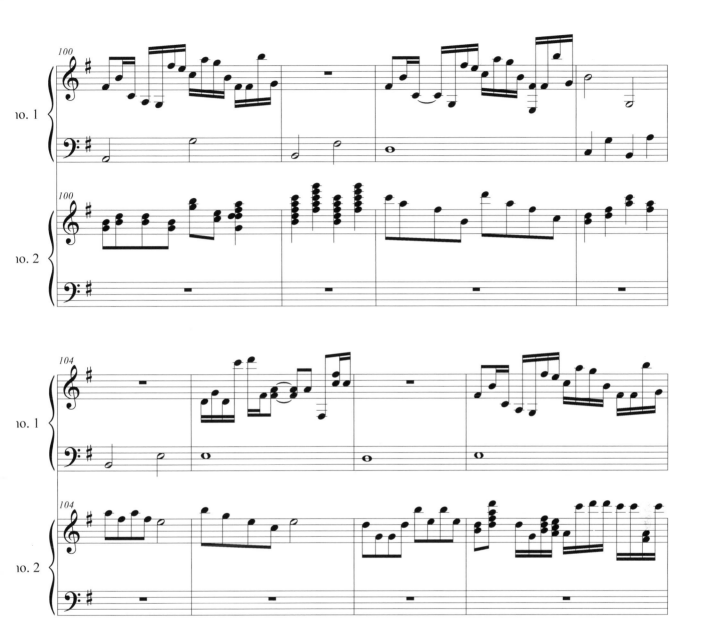

Sonata No 15, Op 70 - Broken Heart

180

Sonata No 15, Op 70 - Broken Heart

Sonata No 15, Op 70 - Broken Heart

Sonata No 15, Op 70 - Broken Heart

186

Sonata No 15, Op 70 - Broken Heart

Sonata No 15, Op 70 - Broken Heart

Sonata No 15, Op 70 - Broken Heart

194

Sonata No 15, Op 70 - Broken Heart

Sonata No 15, Op 70 - Broken Heart

Sonata No 15, Op 70 - Broken Heart

Sonata No 15, Op 70 - Broken Heart

Sonata No 15, Op 70 - Broken Heart

200

Sonata No 15, Op 70 - Broken Heart

Sonata No 15, Op 70 - Broken Heart

Sonata No 15, Op 70 - Broken Heart

Sonata No 15, Op 70 - Broken Heart

206

Sonata No 15, Op 70 - Broken Heart

Sonata No 15, Op 70 - Broken Heart

Sonata No 15, Op 70 - Broken Heart

Sonata No 15, Op 70 - Broken Heart

Sonata No 15, Op 70 - Broken Heart

214

Sonata No 15, Op 70 - Broken Heart

Sonata No 15, Op 70 - Broken Heart

Sonata No 15, Op 70 - Broken Heart

221

Sonata No 15, Op 70 - Broken Heart

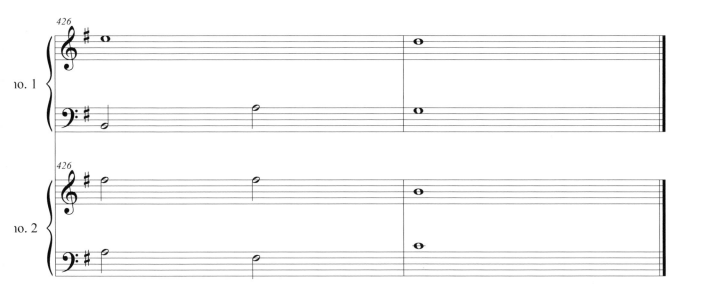

Sonata No 16, Op 72 - Must Be The Higher Power

Dr. Anis I. Milad

Sonata No 16, Op 72 - Must Be The Higher Power

Sonata No 16, Op 72 - Must Be The Higher Power

228

Sonata No 16, Op 72 - Must Be The Higher Power

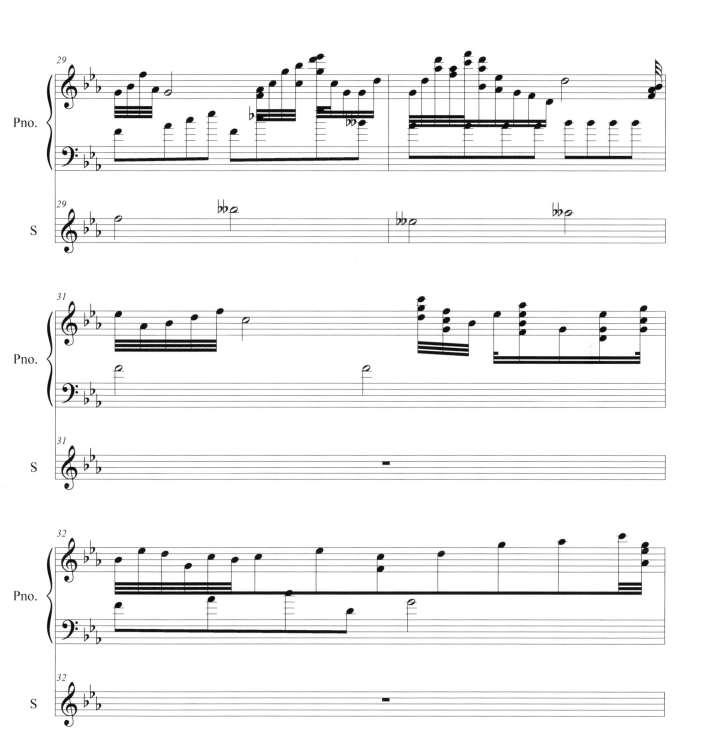

Sonata No 16, Op 72 - Must Be The Higher Power

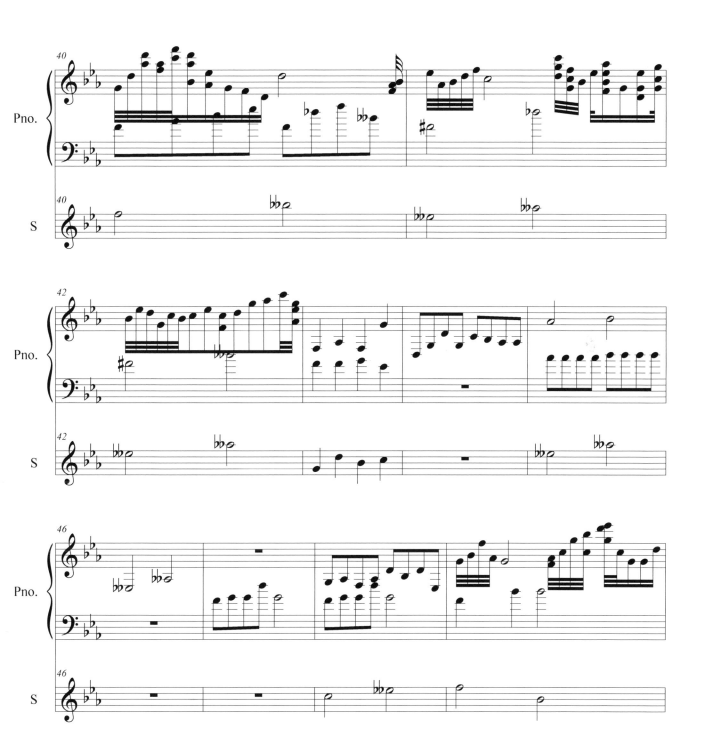

Sonata No 16, Op 72 - Must Be The Higher Power

232

Sonata No 16, Op 72 - Must Be The Higher Power

233

Sonata No 16, Op 72 - Must Be The Higher Power

Sonata No 16, Op 72 - Must Be The Higher Power

Sonata No 16, Op 72 - Must Be The Higher Power

242

Sonata No 16, Op 72 - Must Be The Higher Power

Sonata No 16, Op 72 - Must Be The Higher Power

250

Sonata No 16, Op 72 - Must Be The Higher Power

Sonata No 16, Op 72 - Must Be The Higher Power

253

Sonata No 16, Op 72 - Must Be The Higher Power

Sonata No 16, Op 72 - Must Be The Higher Power

Sonata No 16, Op 72 - Must Be The Higher Power

Sonata No 16, Op 72 - Must Be The Higher Power

Sonata No 16, Op 72 - Must Be The Higher Power

267

Sonata No 16, Op 72 - Must Be The Higher Power

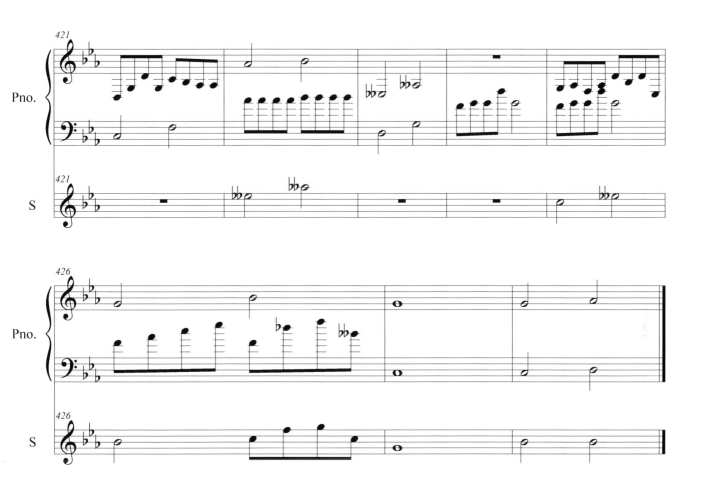

Score

Sonata No 17, Op 74 - Planet 9 Touched Our Generation

Dr. Anis I. Milad

Sonata No 17, Op 74 - Planet 9 Touched Our Generation

274

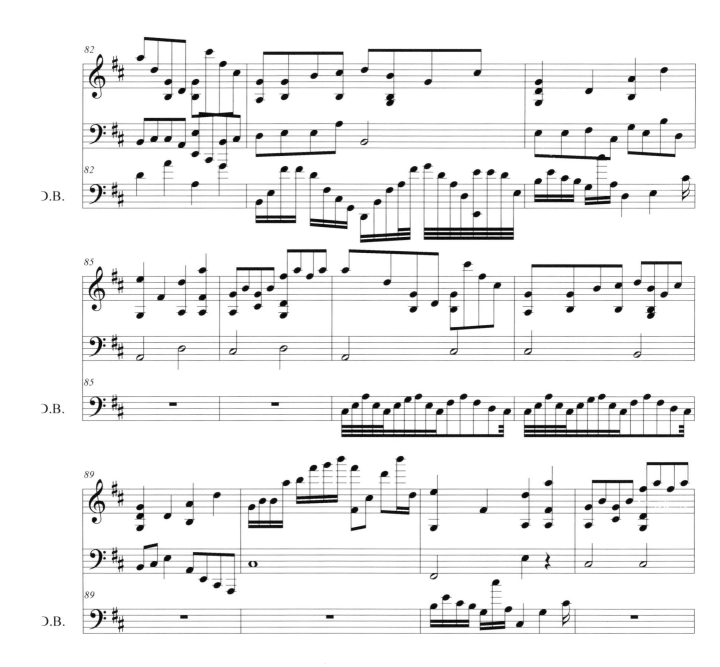

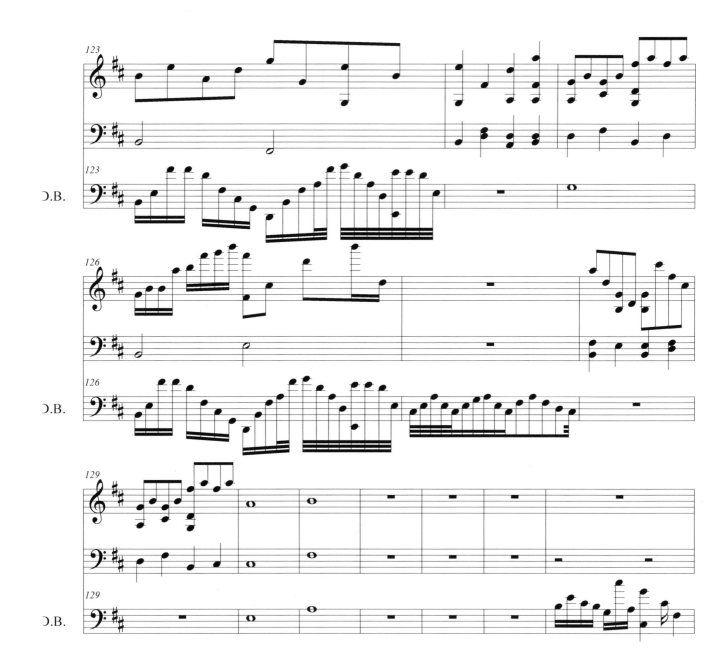

Sonata No 17, Op 74 - Planet 9 Touched Our Generation

Sonata No 17, Op 74 - Planet 9 Touched Our Generation

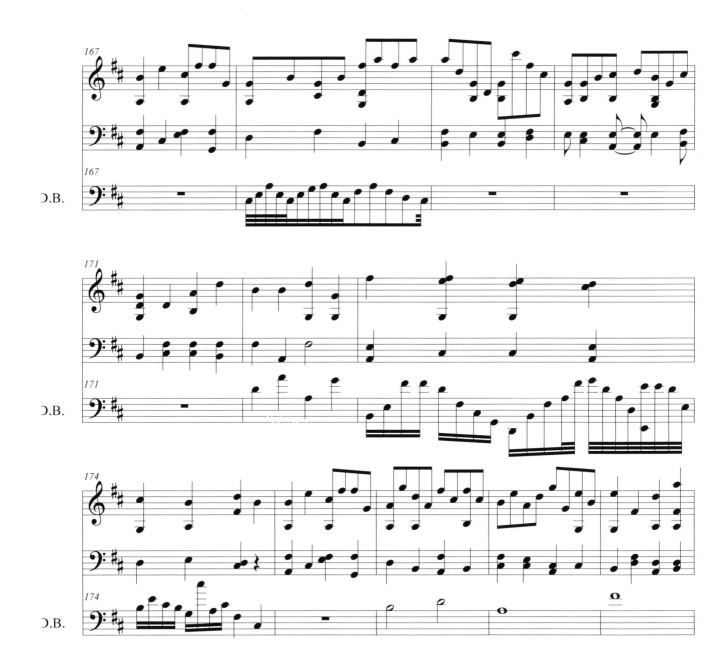

288

Sonata No 17, Op 74 - Planet 9 Touched Our Generation

294

Sonata No 17, Op 74 - Planet 9 Touched Our Generation

Sonata No 17, Op 74 - Planet 9 Touched Our Generation

D.B.

306

Score

Sonata No 18, Op 77 - Earth The Exile of Spirit

Dr. Anis I. milad

Sonata No 18, Op 77 - Earth The Exile of Spirit

Sonata No 18, Op 77 - Earth The Exile of Spirit

Sonata No 18, Op 77 - Earth The Exile of Spirit

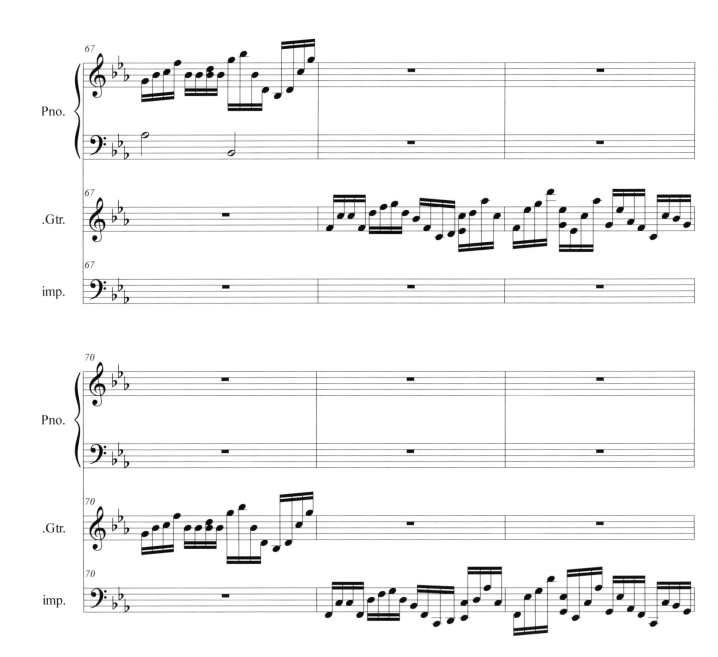

Sonata No 18, Op 77 - Earth The Exile of Spirit

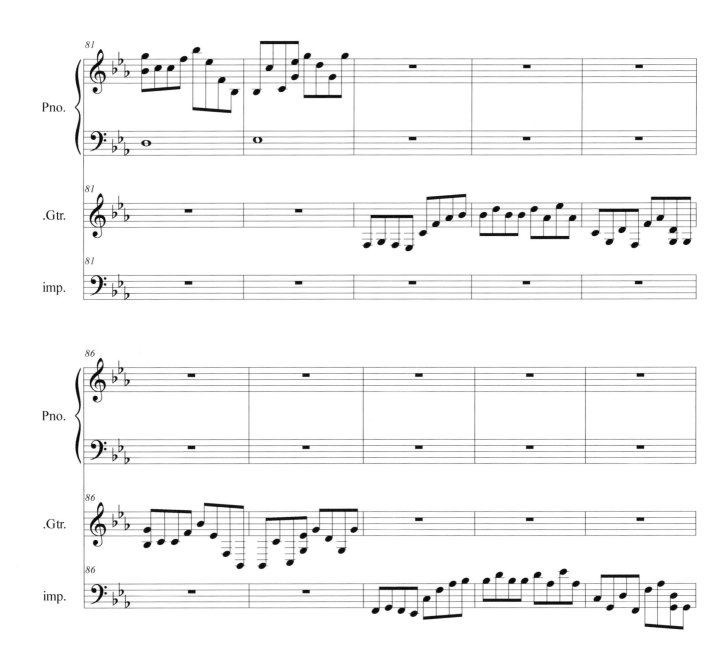

Sonata No 18, Op 77 - Earth The Exile of Spirit

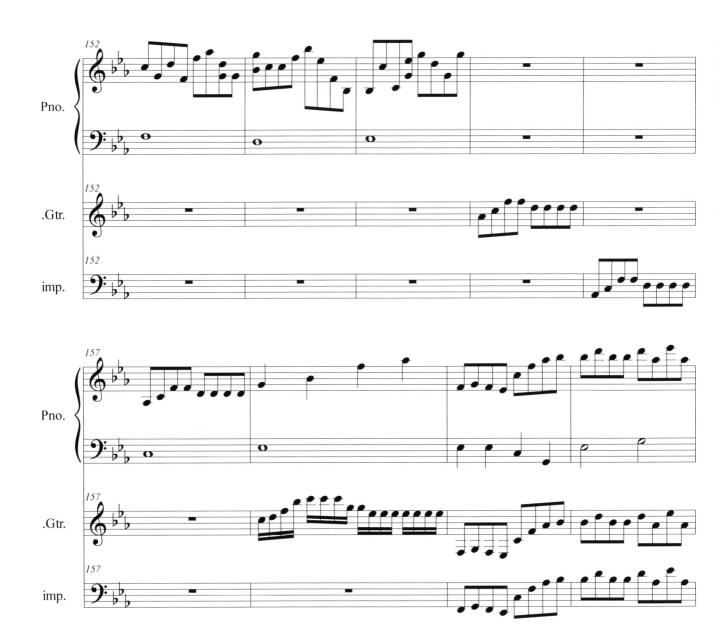

Sonata No 18, Op 77 - Earth The Exile of Spirit

Sonata No 18, Op 77 - Earth The Exile of Spirit

Sonata No 18, Op 77 - Earth The Exile of Spirit

Sonata No 18, Op 77 - Earth The Exile of Spirit

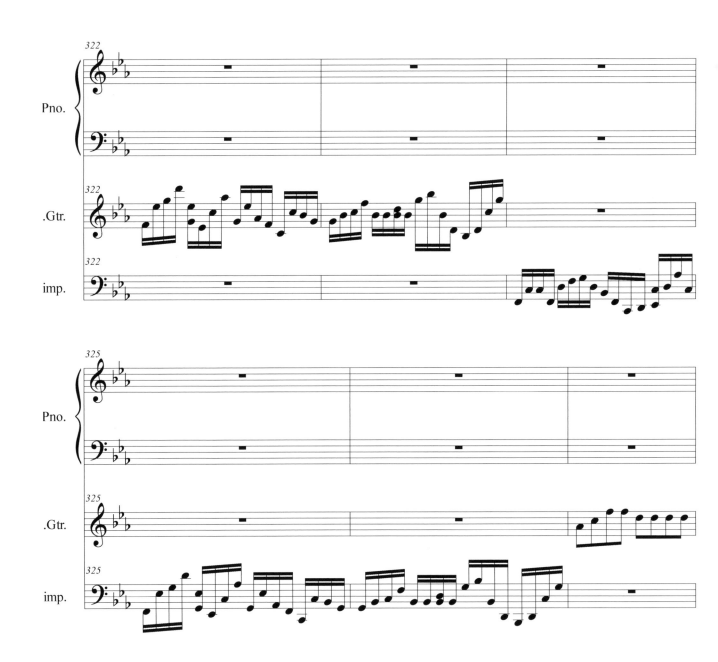

Sonata No 18, Op 77 - Earth The Exile of Spirit

Sonata No 18, Op 77 - Earth The Exile of Spirit

Sonata No 18, Op 77 - Earth The Exile of Spirit

Sonata No 18, Op 77 - Earth The Exile of Spirit

354

Sonata No 18, Op 77 - Earth The Exile of Spirit

Pno.

.Gtr.

imp.

Sonata No 19, Op 78 - The Desert Mirage

Dr. Anis I. Milad

Sonata No 19, Op 78 - The Desert Mirage

Sonata No 19, Op 78 - The Desert Mirage

Sonata No 19, Op 78 - The Desert Mirage

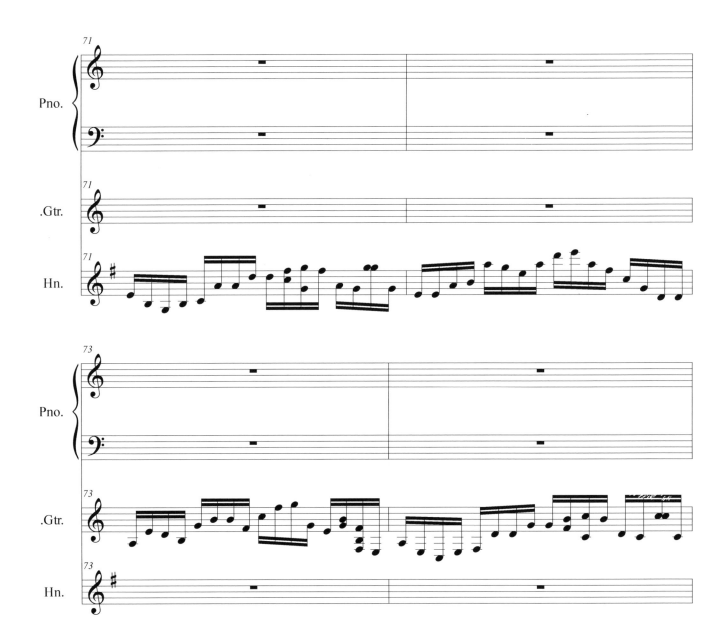

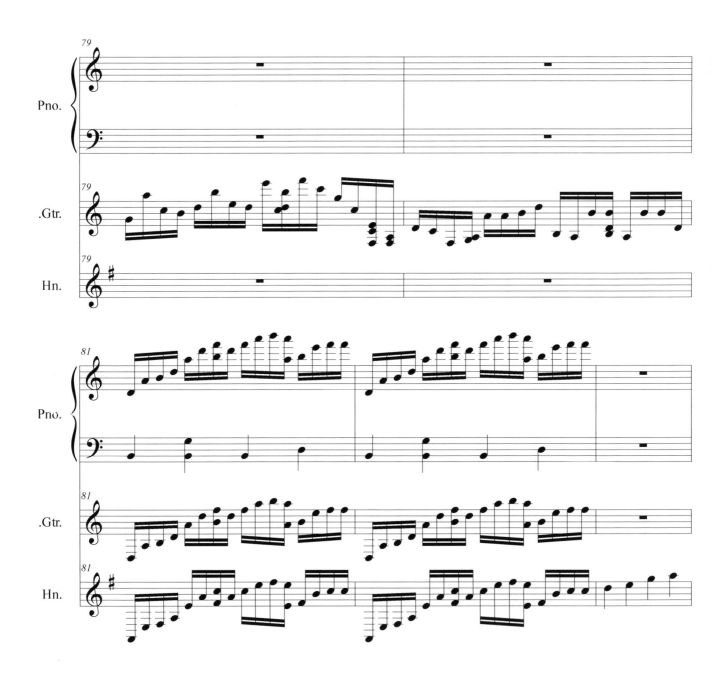

Sonata No 19, Op 78 - The Desert Mirage

Sonata No 19, Op 78 - The Desert Mirage

Sonata No 19, Op 78 - The Desert Mirage

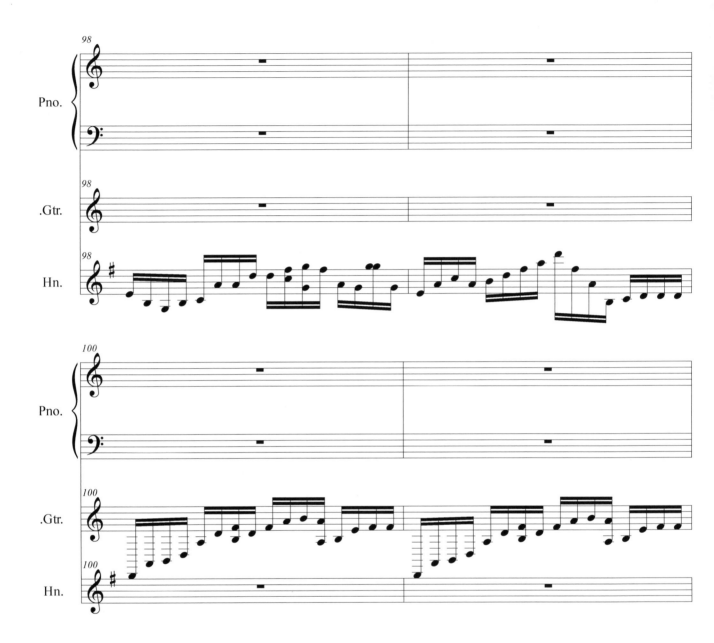

Sonata No 19, Op 78 - The Desert Mirage

Sonata No 19, Op 78 - The Desert Mirage

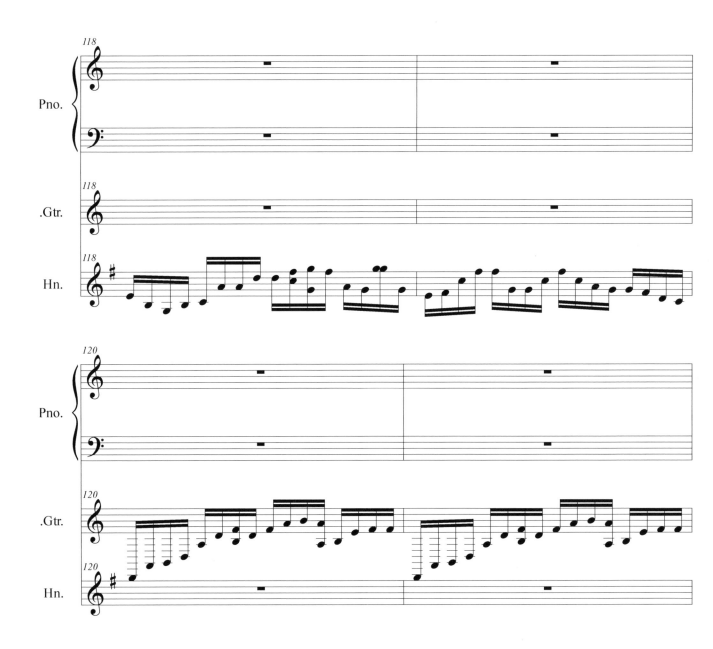

Sonata No 19, Op 78 - The Desert Mirage

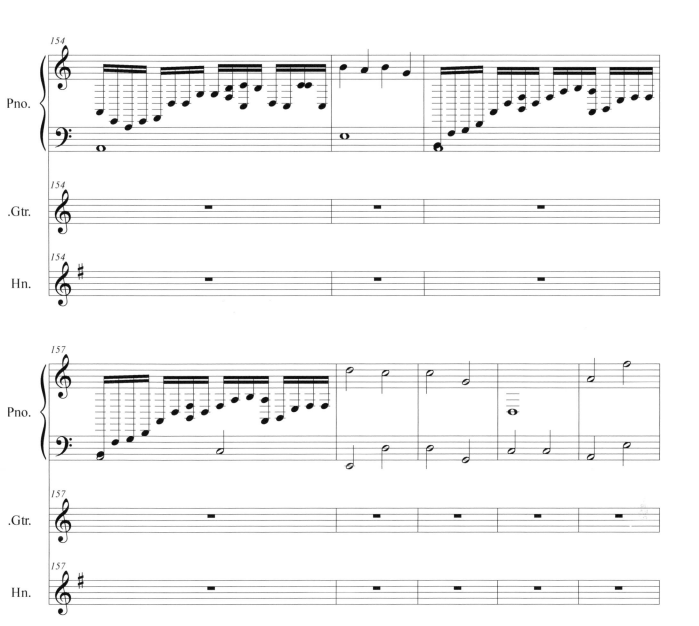

Sonata No 19, Op 78 - The Desert Mirage

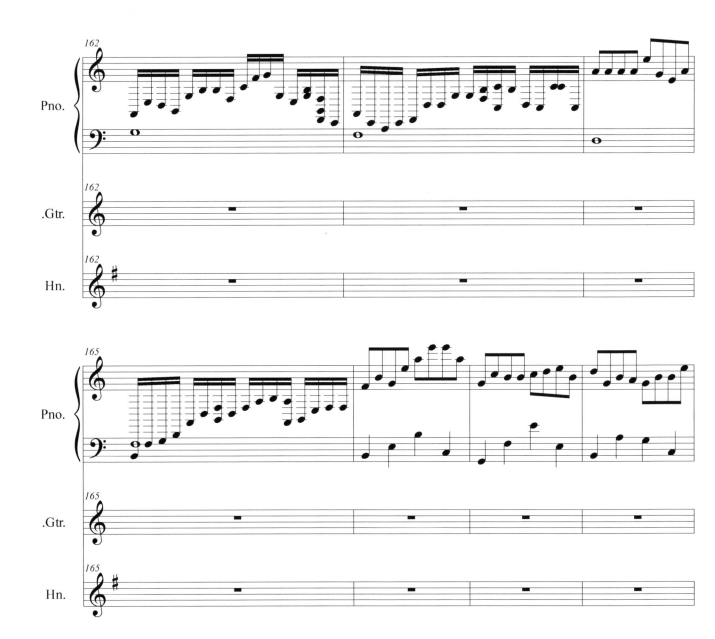

390

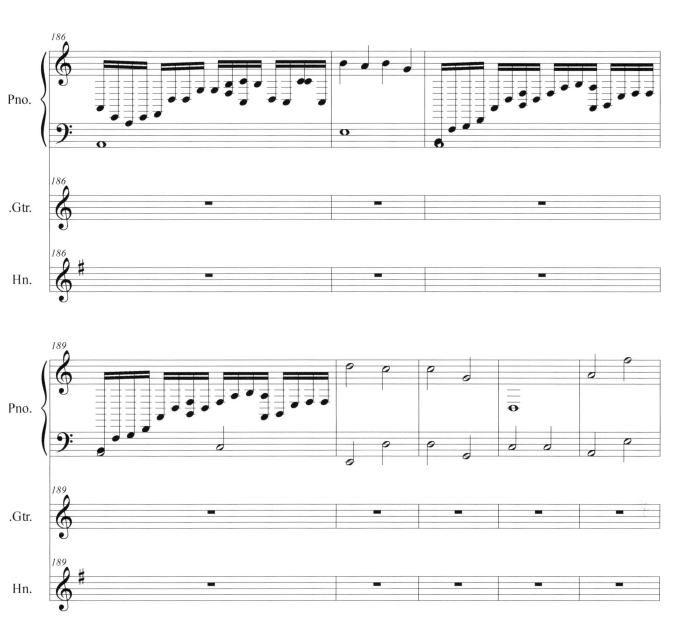

Sonata No 19, Op 78 - The Desert Mirage

Sonata No 19, Op 78 - The Desert Mirage

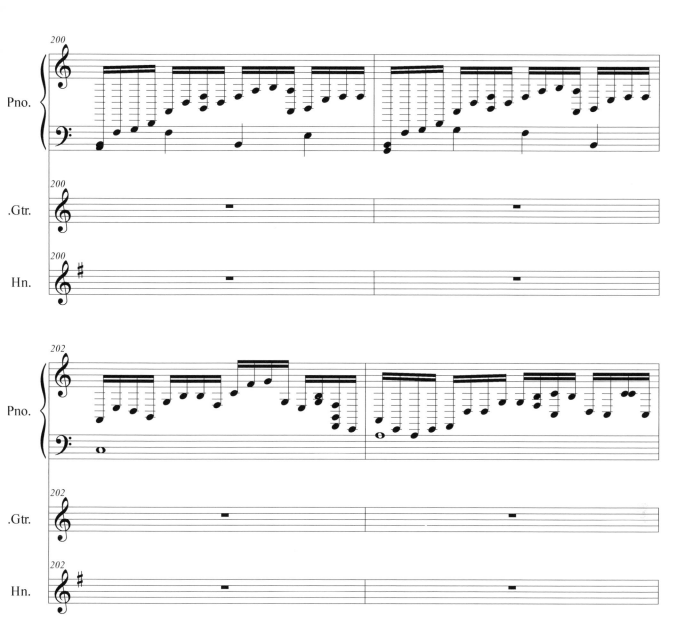

Sonata No 19, Op 78 - The Desert Mirage

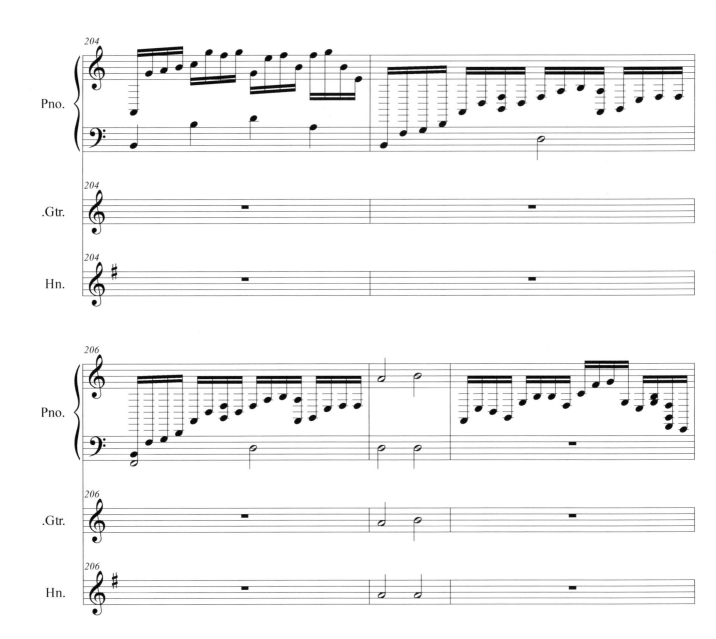

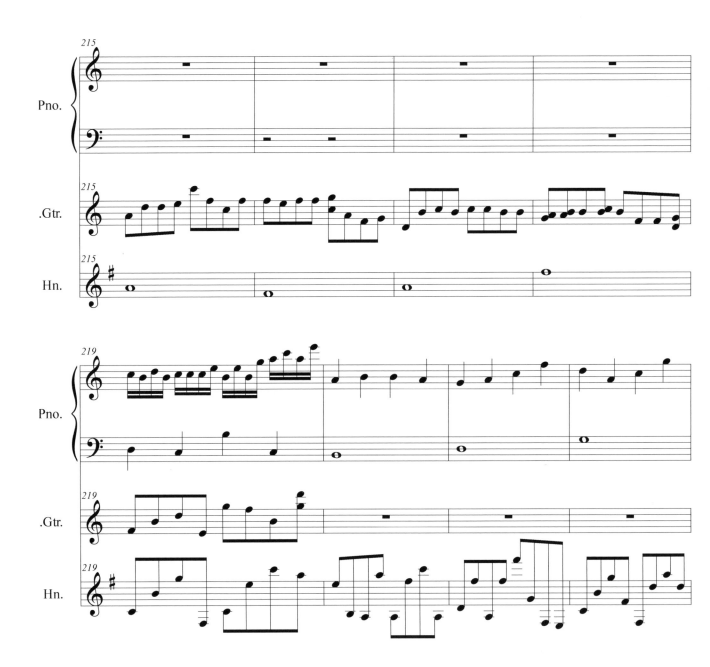

Sonata No 19, Op 78 - The Desert Mirage

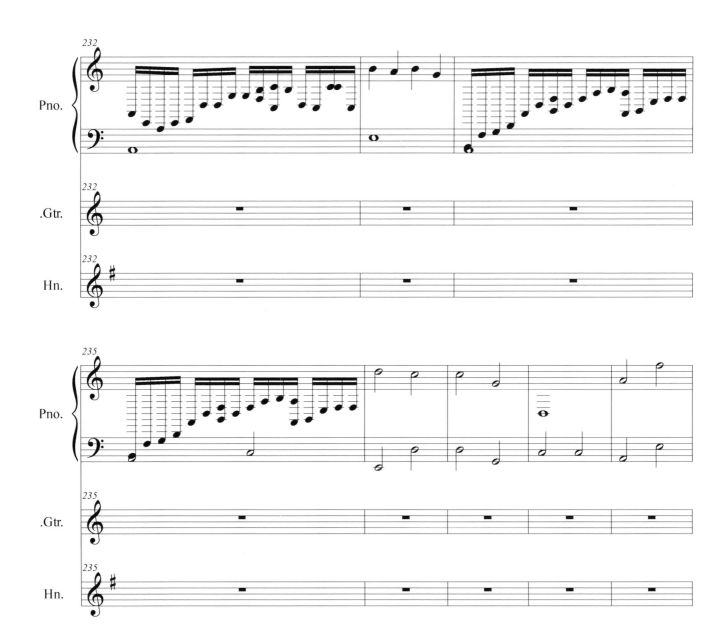

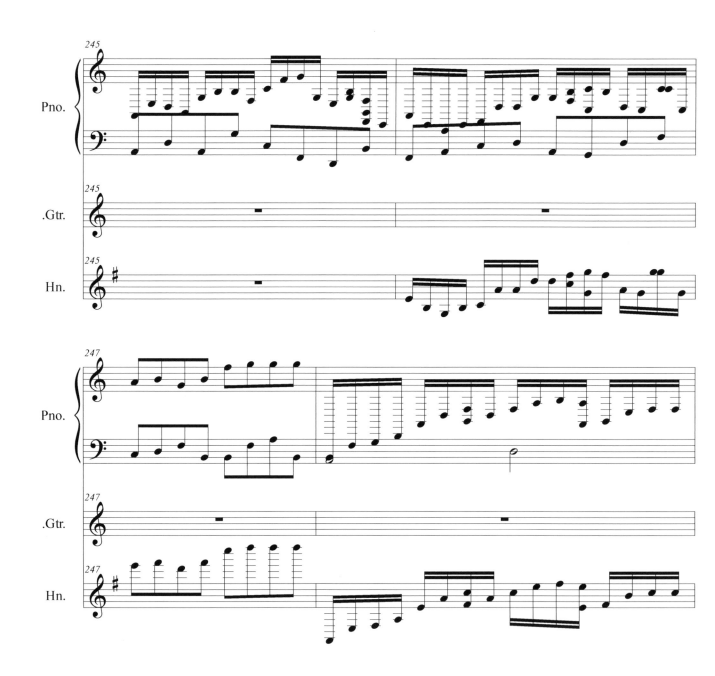

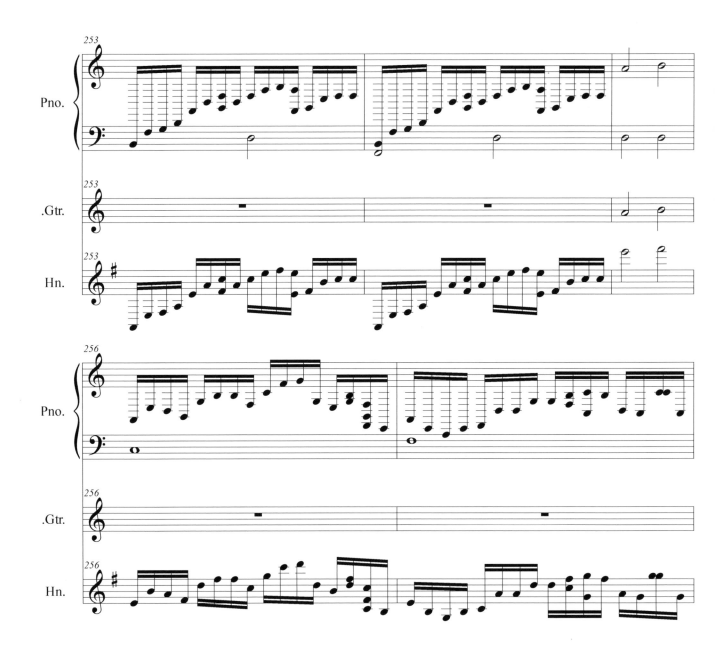

Sonata No 19, Op 78 - The Desert Mirage

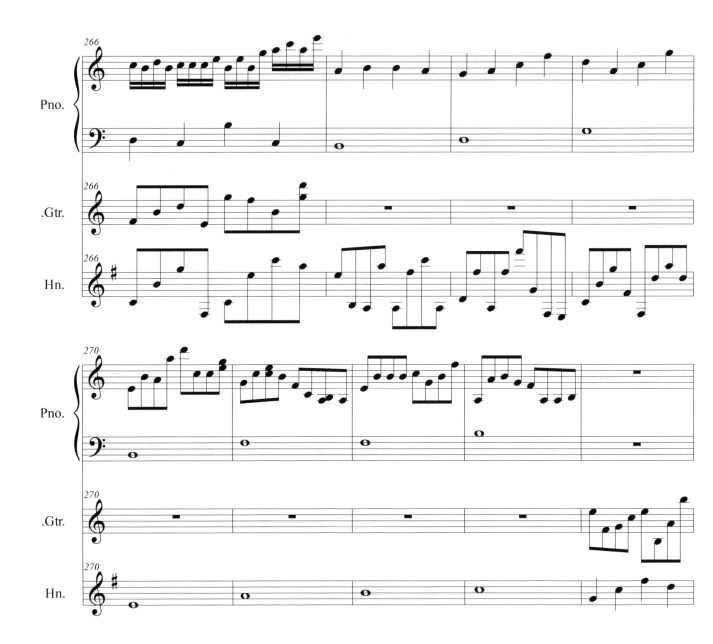

Sonata No 19, Op 78 - The Desert Mirage

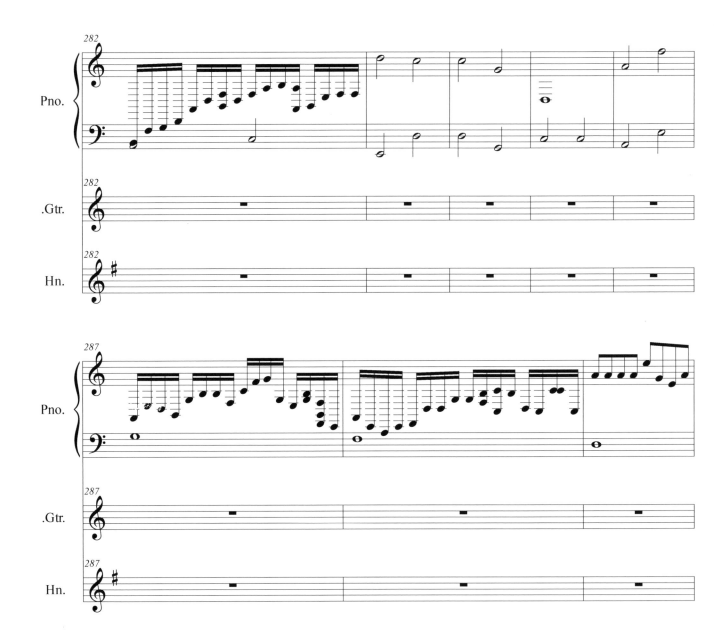

408

Sonata No 19, Op 78 - The Desert Mirage

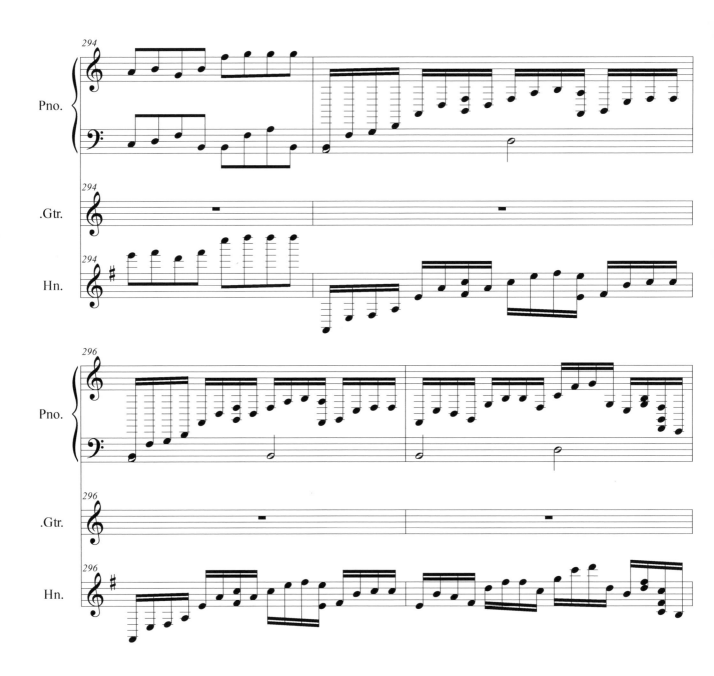

410

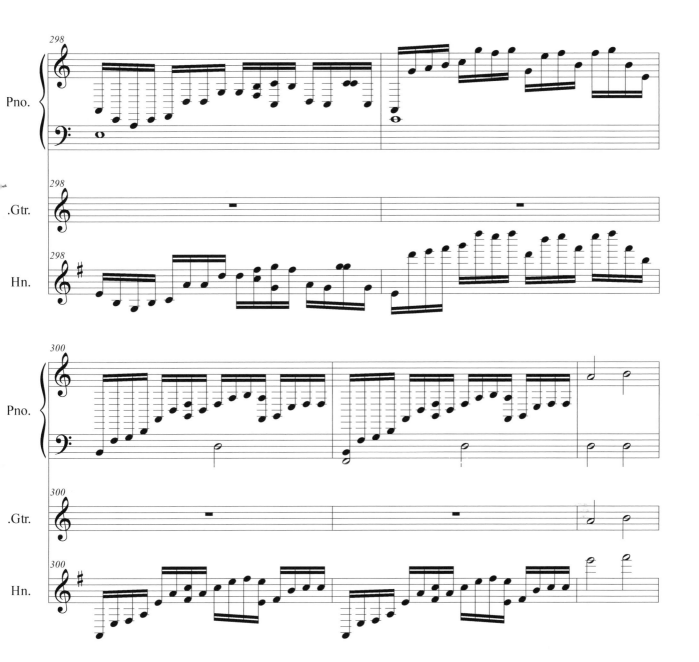

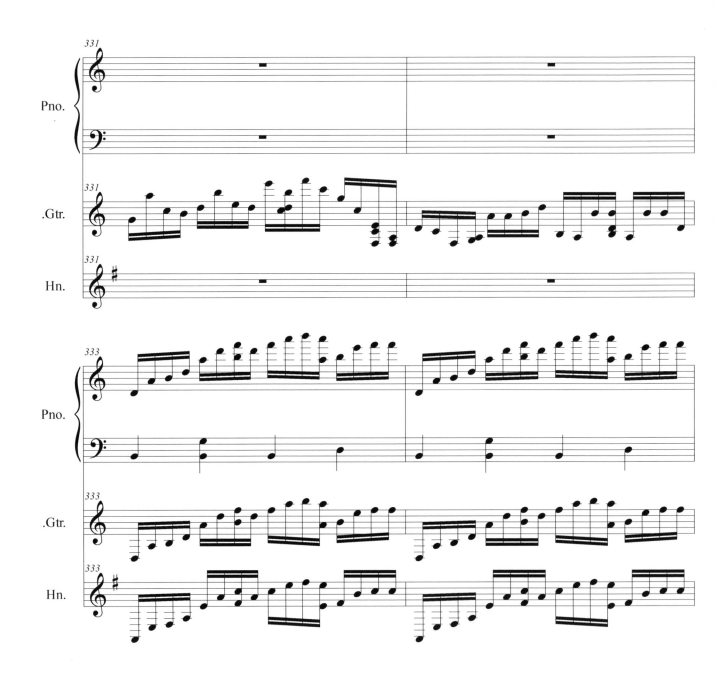

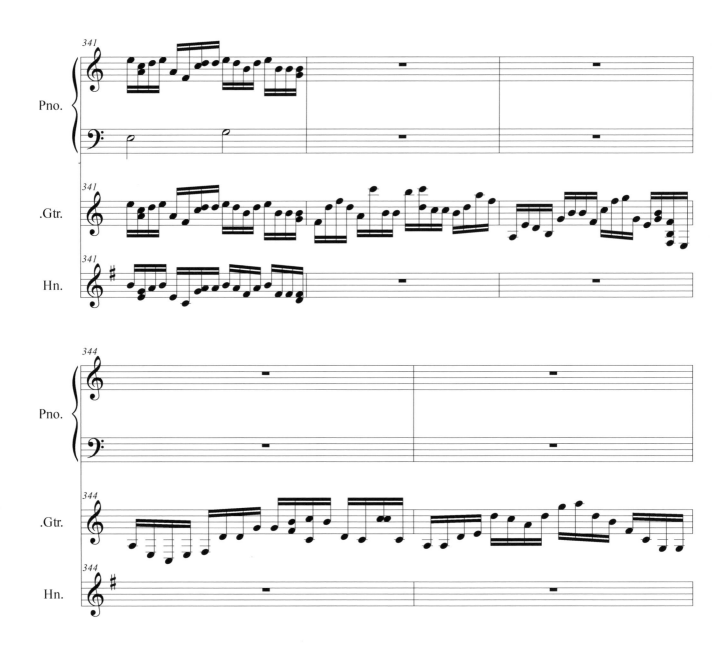

Sonata No 19, Op 78 - The Desert Mirage

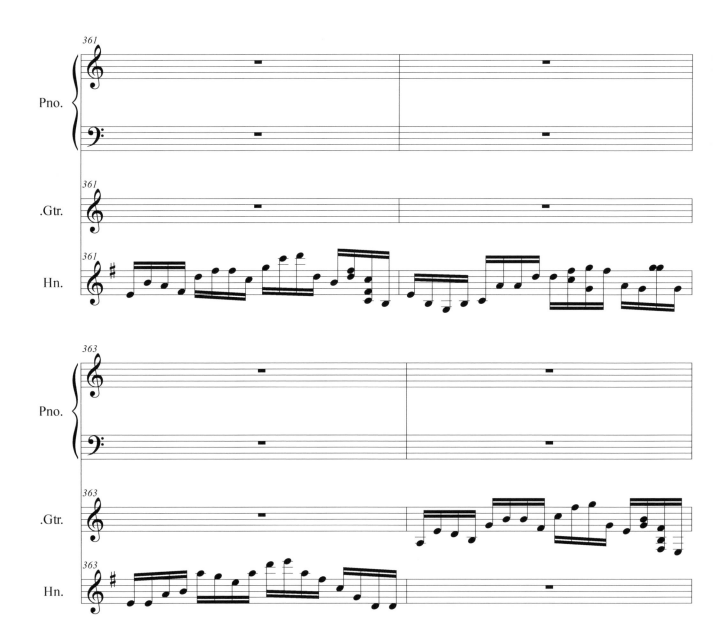

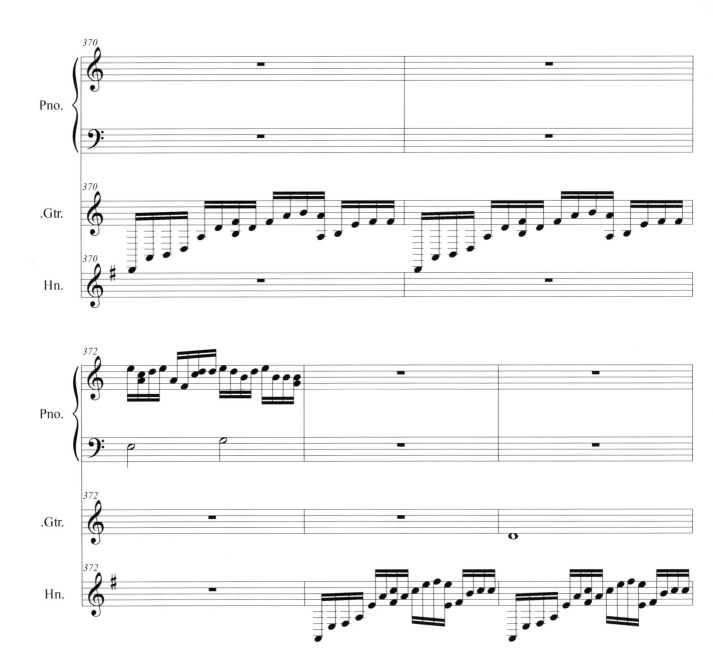

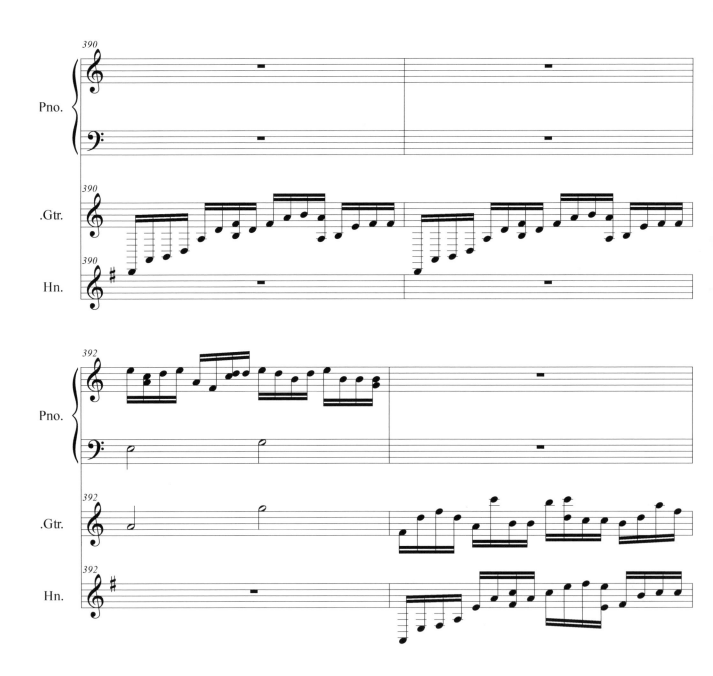

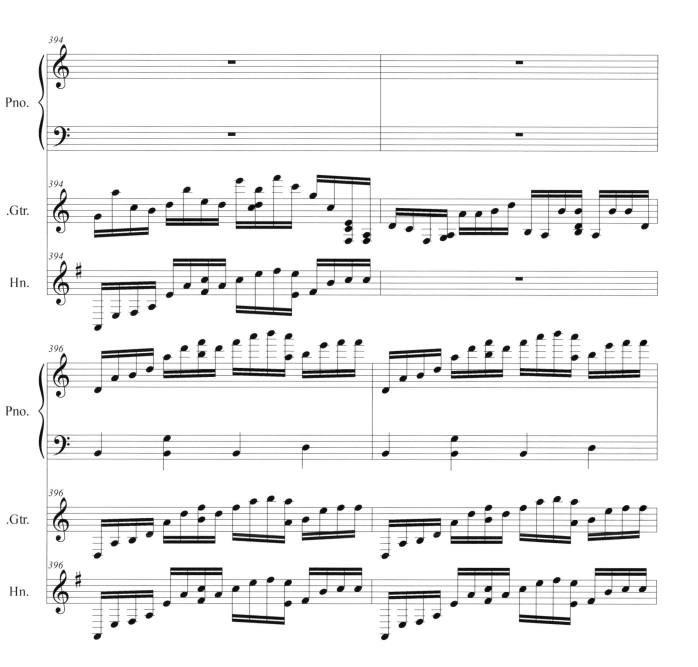

Sonata No 19, Op 78 - The Desert Mirage

430

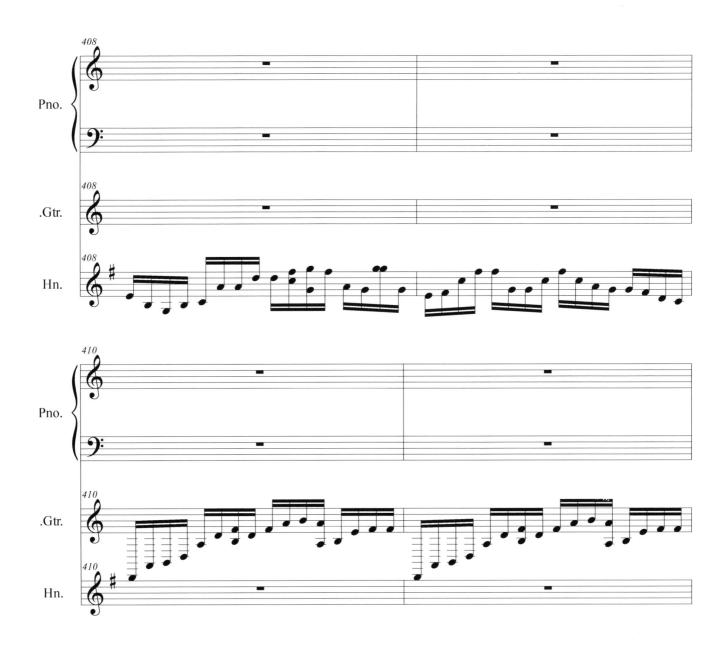

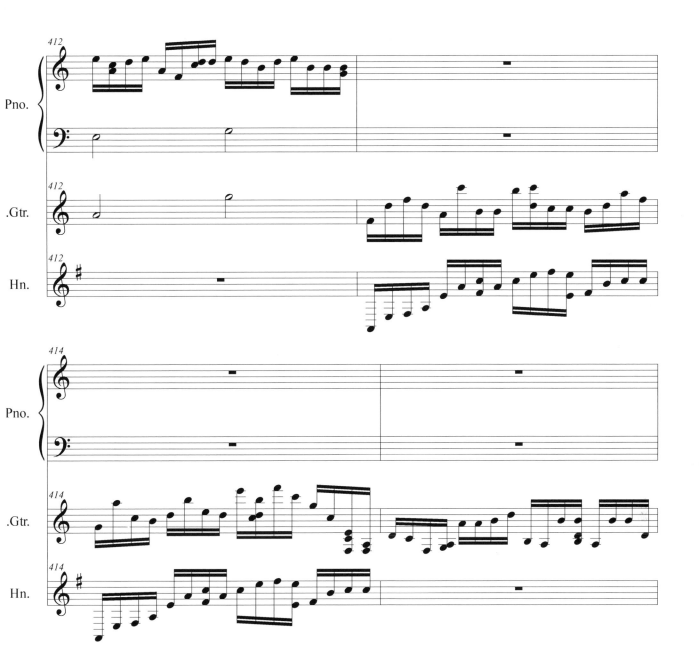

Sonata No 19, Op 78 - The Desert Mirage

Sonata No 20, Op 79 - Sadness in Egypt

Dr. Anis I. Milad

Sonata No 20, Op 79 - Sadness in Egypt

Sonata No 20, Op 79 - Sadness in Egypt

Sonata No 20, Op 79 - Sadness in Egypt

440

Sonata No 20, Op 79 - Sadness in Egypt

Sonata No 20, Op 79 - Sadness in Egypt

Sonata No 20, Op 79 - Sadness in Egypt

Sonata No 20, Op 79 - Sadness in Egypt

449

Sonata No 20, Op 79 - Sadness in Egypt

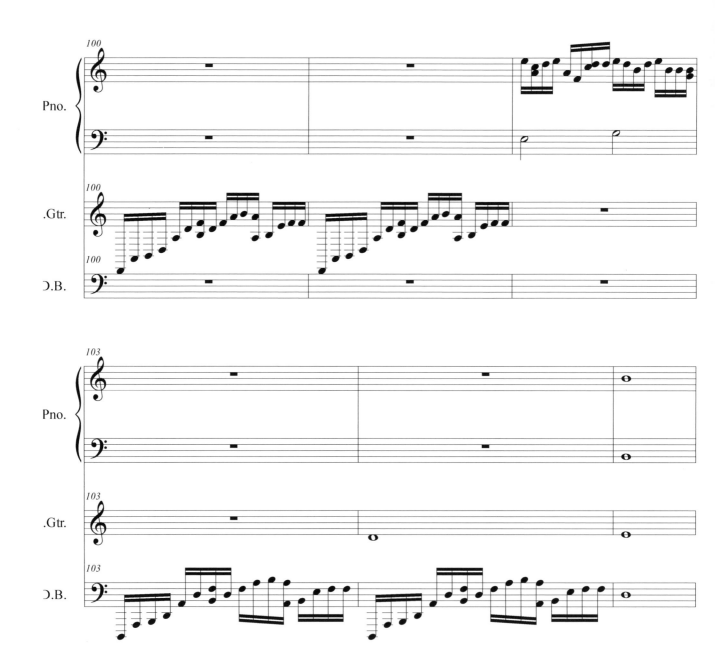

Sonata No 20, Op 79 - Sadness in Egypt

Sonata No 20, Op 79 - Sadness in Egypt

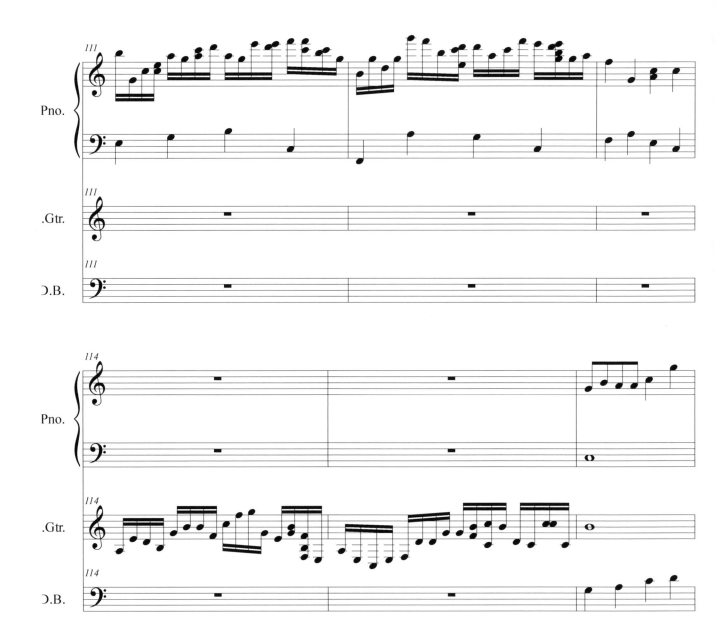

Sonata No 20, Op 79 - Sadness in Egypt

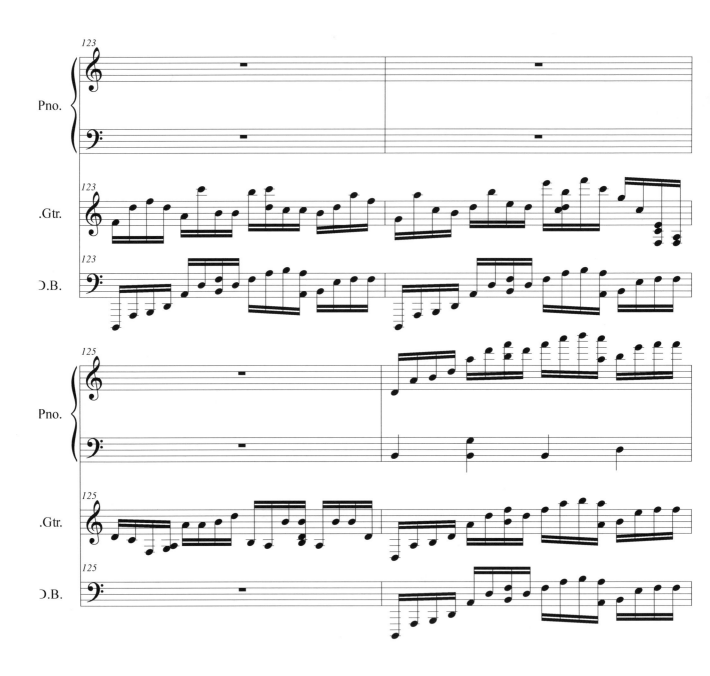

Sonata No 20, Op 79 - Sadness in Egypt

Sonata No 20, Op 79 - Sadness in Egypt

Sonata No 20, Op 79 - Sadness in Egypt

461

Sonata No 20, Op 79 - Sadness in Egypt

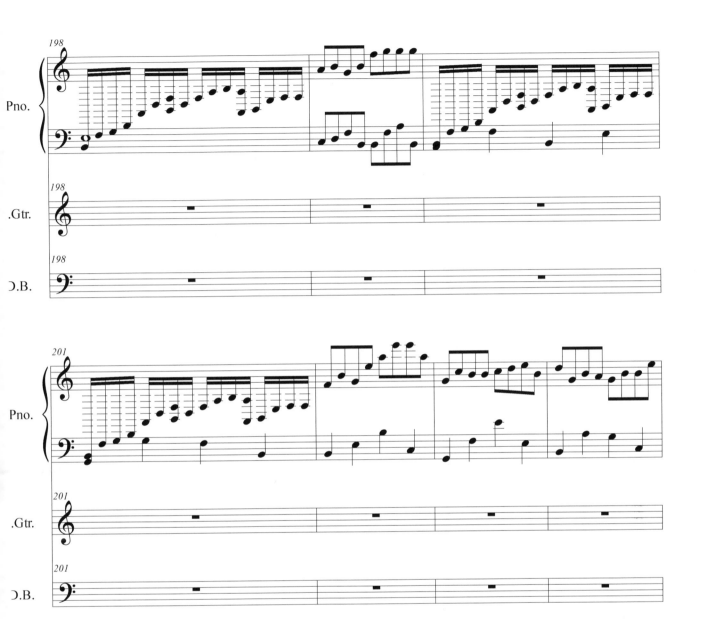

Sonata No 20, Op 79 - Sadness in Egypt

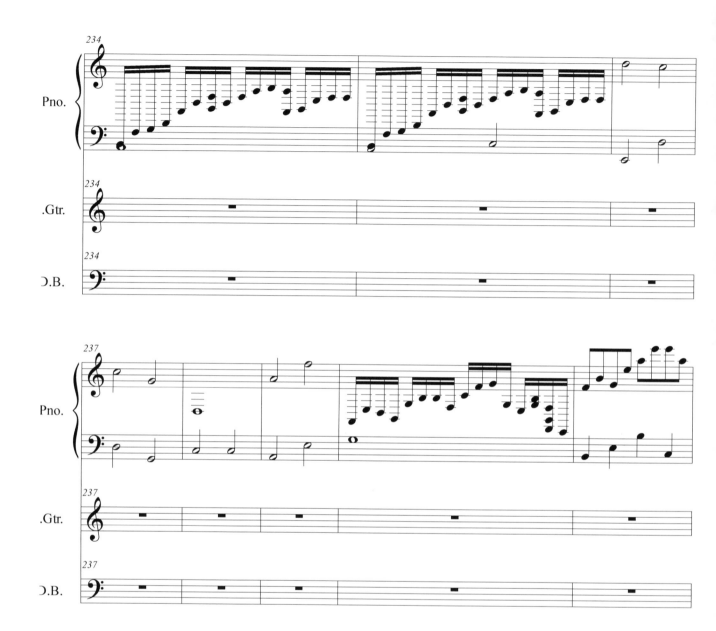

Sonata No 20, Op 79 - Sadness in Egypt

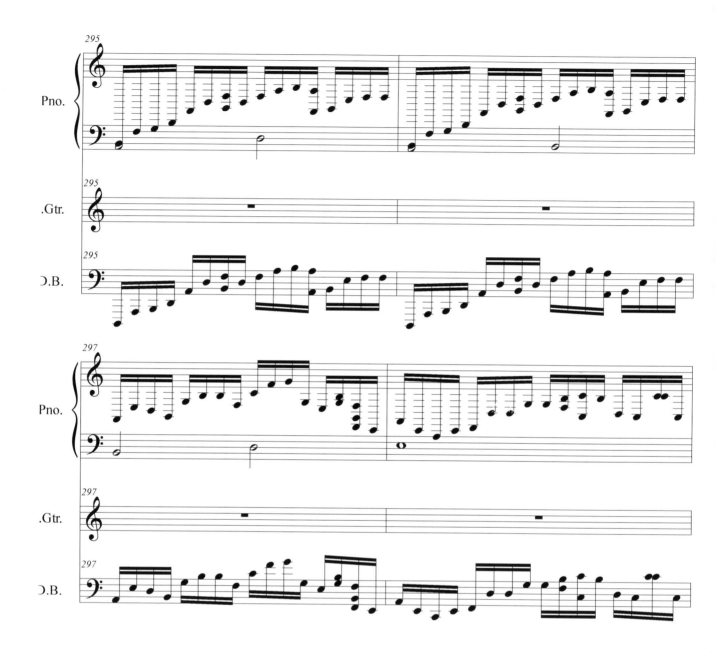

Sonata No 20, Op 79 - Sadness in Egypt

480

Sonata No 20, Op 79 - Sadness in Egypt

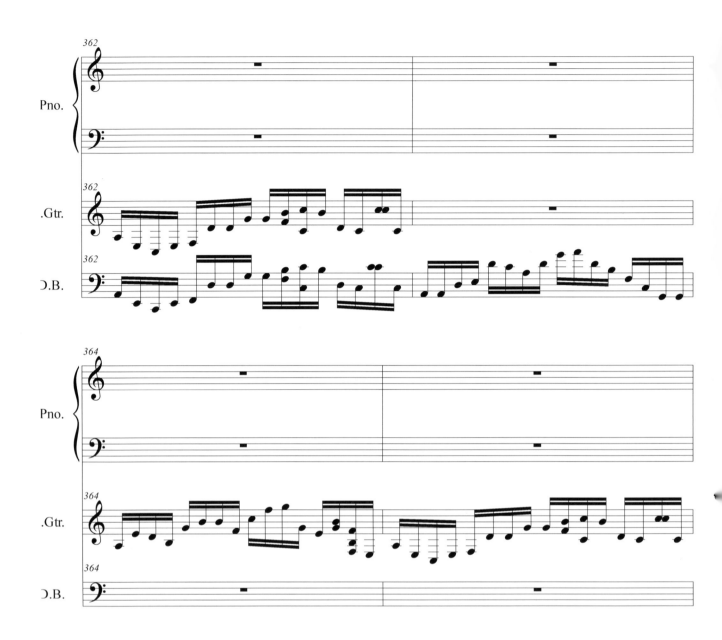

Sonata No 20, Op 79 - Sadness in Egypt

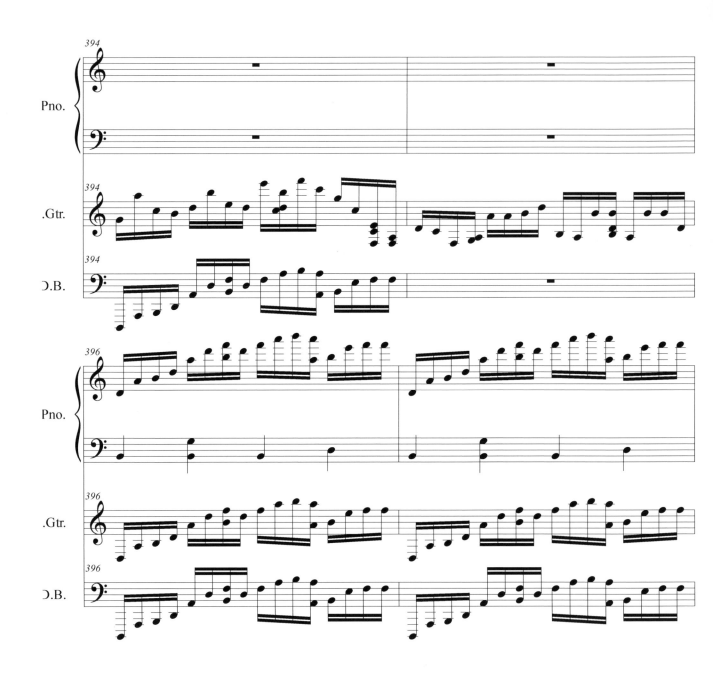

Sonata No 20, Op 79 - Sadness in Egypt

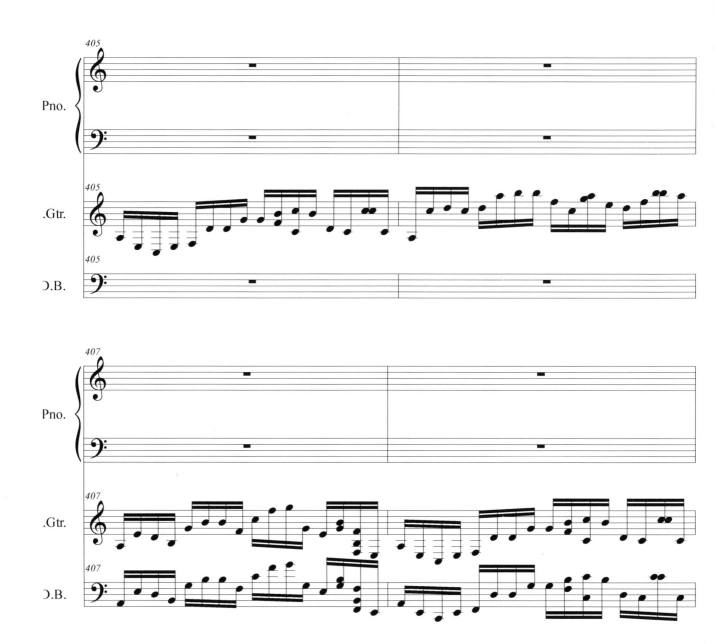

Sonata No 20, Op 79 - Sadness in Egypt